RENASCENCE

RENASCENCE

AND

OTHER POEMS

BY

EDNA ST. VINCENT MILLAY

PUBLISHERS

HARPER & BROTHERS

NEW YORK AND LONDON

RENASCENCE

ALL I could see from where I stood
Was three long mountains and a wood;
I turned and looked the other way,
And saw three islands in a bay.
So with my eyes I traced the line
Of the horizon, thin and fine,
Straight around till I was come
Back to where I'd started from;
And all I saw from where I stood
Was three long mountains and a wood.
Over these things I could not see:
These were the things that bounded me;

And I could touch them with my hand,

Almost, I thought, from where I stand.

And all at once things seemed so small

My breath came short, and scarce at all.

But, sure, the sky is big, I said;

Miles and miles above my head;

So here upon my back I'll lie

And look my fill into the sky.

And so I looked, and, after all,

The sky was not so very tall.

The sky, I said, must somewhere stop,

And—sure enough!—I see the top!

The sky, I thought, is not so grand;

I 'most could touch it with my hand!

And reaching up my hand to try,

I screamed to feel it touch the sky.

RENASCENCE

I screamed, and—lo!—Infinity

Came down and settled over me;

Forced back my scream into my chest,

Bent back my arm upon my breast,

And, pressing of the Undefined

The definition on my mind,

Held up before my eyes a glass

Through which my shrinking sight did pass

Until it seemed I must behold

Immensity made manifold;

Whispered to me a word whose sound

Deafened the air for worlds around,

And brought unmuffled to my ears

The gossiping of friendly spheres,

The creaking of the tented sky,

The ticking of Eternity.

I saw and heard and knew at last

The How and Why of all things, past,

And present, and forevermore.

The Universe, cleft to the core,

Lay open to my probing sense

That, sick'ning, I would fain pluck thence

But could not,—nay! But needs must suck

At the great wound, and could not pluck

My lips away till I had drawn

All venom out.—Ah, fearful pawn!

For my omniscience paid I toll

In infinite remorse of soul.

All sin was of my sinning, all

Atoning mine, and mine the gall

Of all regret. Mine was the weight

Of every brooded wrong, the hate

4

That stood behind each envious thrust,

Mine every greed, mine every lust.

And all the while for every grief,

Each suffering, I craved relief

With individual desire,—

Craved all in vain! And felt fierce fire

About a thousand people crawl;

Perished with each,—then mourned for all!

A man was starving in Capri;

He moved his eyes and looked at me;

I felt his gaze, I heard his moan,

And knew his hunger as my own.

I saw at sea a great fog bank

Between two ships that struck and sank;

A thousand screams the heavens smote;

And every scream tore through my throat.

No hurt I did not feel, no death

That was not mine; mine each last breath

That, crying, met an answering cry

From the compassion that was I.

All suffering mine, and mine its rod;

Mine, pity like the pity of God.

Ah, awful weight! Infinity

Pressed down upon the finite Me!

My anguished spirit, like a bird,

Beating against my lips I heard;

Yet lay the weight so close about

There was no room for it without.

And so beneath the weight lay I

And suffered death, but could not die.

Long had I lain thus, craving death,

When quietly the earth beneath
Gave way, and inch by inch, so great
At last had grown the crushing weight,
Into the earth I sank till I
Full six feet under ground did lie,
And sank no more,—there is no weight
Can follow here, however great.
From off my breast I felt it roll,
And as it went my tortured soul
Burst forth and fled in such a gust
That all about me swirled the dust.

Deep in the earth I rested now;
Cool is its hand upon the brow
And soft its breast beneath the head
Of one who is so gladly dead.

7

And all at once, and over all

The pitying rain began to fall;

I lay and heard each pattering hoof

Upon my lowly, thatchèd roof,

And seemed to love the sound far more

Than ever I had done before.

For rain it hath a friendly sound

To one who's six feet under ground;

And scarce the friendly voice or face:

A grave is such a quiet place.

The rain, I said, is kind to come

And speak to me in my new home.

I would I were alive again

To kiss the fingers of the rain,

To drink into my eyes the shine

Of every slanting silver line,

To catch the freshened, fragrant breeze

From drenched and dripping apple-trees.

For soon the shower will be done,

And then the broad face of the sun

Will laugh above the rain-soaked earth

Until the world with answering mirth

Shakes joyously, and each round drop

Rolls, twinkling, from its grass-blade top.

How can I bear it; buried here,

While overhead the sky grows clear

And blue again after the storm?

O, multi-colored, multiform,

Beloved beauty over me,

That I shall never, never see

Again! Spring-silver, autumn-gold,

That I shall never more behold!

Sleeping your myriad magics through,

Close-sepulchred away from you!

O God, I cried, give me new birth,

And put me back upon the earth!

Upset each cloud's gigantic gourd

And let the heavy rain, down-poured

In one big torrent, set me free,

Washing my grave away from me!

I ceased; and through the breathless hush

That answered me, the far-off rush

Of herald wings came whispering

Like music down the vibrant string

Of my ascending prayer, and—crash!

Before the wild wind's whistling lash

The startled storm-clouds reared on high

And plunged in terror down the sky,

And the big rain in one black wave

Fell from the sky and struck my grave.

I know not how such things can be;

I only know there came to me

A fragrance such as never clings

To aught save happy living things;

A sound as of some joyous elf

Singing sweet songs to please himself,

And, through and over everything,

A sense of glad awakening.

The grass, a-tiptoe at my ear,

Whispering to me I could hear;

I felt the rain's cool finger-tips

Brushed tenderly across my lips,

Laid gently on my sealèd sight,

And all at once the heavy night

Fell from my eyes and I could see,—

A drenched and dripping apple-tree,

A last long line of silver rain,

A sky grown clear and blue again.

And as I looked a quickening gust

Of wind blew up to me and thrust

Into my face a miracle

Of orchard-breath, and with the smell,—

I know not how such things can be!—

I breathed my soul back into me.

Ah! Up then from the ground sprang I

And hailed the earth with such a cry

As is not heard save from a man

Who has been dead, and lives again.

About the trees my arms I wound;

Like one gone mad I hugged the ground;

I raised my quivering arms on high;

I laughed and laughed into the sky,

Till at my throat a strangling sob

Caught fiercely, and a great heart-throb

Sent instant tears into my eyes;

O God, I cried, no dark disguise

Can e'er hereafter hide from me

Thy radiant identity!

Thou canst not move across the grass

But my quick eyes will see Thee pass,

Nor speak, however silently,

But my hushed voice will answer Thee.

I know the path that tells Thy way

Through the cool eve of every day;

God, I can push the grass apart
And lay my finger on Thy heart!

The world stands out on either side
No wider than the heart is wide;
Above the world is stretched the sky,—
No higher than the soul is high.
The heart can push the sea and land
Farther away on either hand;
The soul can split the sky in two,
And let the face of God shine through.
But East and West will pinch the heart
That can not keep them pushed apart;
And he whose soul is flat—the sky
Will cave in on him by and by.

INTERIM

The room is full of you!—As I came in
And closed the door behind me, all at once
A something in the air, intangible,
Yet stiff with meaning, struck my senses sick!—

Sharp, unfamiliar odors have destroyed
Each other room's dear personality.
The heavy scent of damp, funereal flowers,—
The very essence, hush-distilled, of Death—
Has strangled that habitual breath of home
Whose expiration leaves all houses dead;

15

And wheresoe'er I look is hideous change.

Save here. Here 'twas as if a weed-choked gate

Had opened at my touch, and I had stepped

Into some long-forgot, enchanted, strange,

Sweet garden of a thousand years ago

And suddenly thought, "I have been here before!"

You are not here. I know that you are gone,

And will not ever enter here again.

And yet it seems to me, if I should speak,

Your silent step must wake across the hall;

If I should turn my head, that your sweet eyes

Would kiss me from the door.—So short a time

To teach my life its transposition to

This difficult and unaccustomed key!—

The room is as you left it; your last touch—

A thoughtless pressure, knowing not itself
As saintly—hallows now each simple thing;
Hallows and glorifies, and glows between
The dust's grey fingers like a shielded light.

There is your book, just as you laid it down,
Face to the table,—I cannot believe
That you are gone!—Just then it seemed to me
You must be here.   I almost laughed to think
How like reality the dream had been;
Yet knew before I laughed, and so was still.
That book, outspread, just as you laid it down!
Perhaps you thought, "I wonder what comes next,
And whether this or this will be the end";
So rose, and left it, thinking to return.

Perhaps that chair, when you arose and passed

Out of the room, rocked silently a while

Ere it again was still. When you were gone

Forever from the room, perhaps that chair,

Stirred by your movement, rocked a little while,

Silently, to and fro . . .

And here are the last words your fingers wrote,

Scrawled in broad characters across a page

In this brown book I gave you. Here your hand,

Guiding your rapid pen, moved up and down.

Here with a looping knot you crossed a "t,"

And here another like it, just beyond

These two eccentric "e's." You were so small,

And wrote so brave a hand!

                              How strange it seems

That of all words these are the words you chose!

And yet a simple choice; you did not know

You would not write again. If you had known—

But then, it does not matter,—and indeed

If you had known there was so little time

You would have dropped your pen and come to me

And this page would be empty, and some phrase

Other than this would hold my wonder now.

Yet, since you could not know, and it befell

That these are the last words your fingers wrote,

There is a dignity some might not see

In this, "I picked the first sweet-pea to-day."

To-day! Was there an opening bud beside it

You left until to-morrow?—O my love,

The things that withered,—and you came not back!

That day you filled this circle of my arms

That now is empty. (O my empty life!)

That day—that day you picked the first sweet-
  pea,—

And brought it in to show me! I recall

With terrible distinctness how the smell

Of your cool gardens drifted in with you.

I know, you held it up for me to see

And flushed because I looked not at the flower,

But at your face; and when behind my look

You saw such unmistakable intent

You laughed and brushed your flower against my
  lips.

(You were the fairest thing God ever made,

I think.) And then your hands above my heart

Drew down its stem into a fastening,

And while your head was bent I kissed your hair.

I wonder if you knew.   (Beloved hands!

Somehow I cannot seem to see them still.

Somehow I cannot seem to see the dust

In your bright hair.)   What is the need of Heaven

When earth can be so sweet?—If only God

Had let us love,—and show the world the way!

Strange cancellings must ink th' eternal books

When love-crossed-out will bring the answer right!

That first sweet-pea!   I wonder where it is.

It seems to me I laid it down somewhere,

And yet,—I am not sure.   I am not sure,

Even, if it was white or pink; for then

'Twas much like any other flower to me,

Save that it was the first.   I did not know,

Then, that it was the last.   If I had known—

But then, it does not matter.   Strange how few,

21

After all's said and done, the things that are
Of moment.

    Few indeed! When I can make
Of ten small words a rope to hang the world!
"I had you and I have you now no more."
There, there it dangles,—where's the little truth
That can for long keep footing under that
When its slack syllables tighten to a thought?
Here, let me write it down! I wish to see
Just how a thing like that will look on paper!

"I had you and I have you now no more."

O little words, how can you run so straight
Across the page, beneath the weight you bear?
How can you fall apart, whom such a theme

Has bound together, and hereafter aid

In trivial expression, that have been

So hideously dignified?—Would God

That tearing you apart would tear the thread

I strung you on! Would God—O God, my mind

Stretches asunder on this merciless rack

Of imagery! O, let me sleep a while!

Would I could sleep, and wake to find me back

In that sweet summer afternoon with you.

Summer? 'Tis summer still by the calendar!

How easily could God, if He so willed,

Set back the world a little turn or two!

Correct its griefs, and brings its joys again!

We were so wholly one I had not thought

That we could die apart. I had not thought

That I could move,—and you be stiff and still!

That I could speak,—and you perforce be dumb!

I think our heart-strings were, like warp and woof

In some firm fabric, woven in and out;

Your golden filaments in fair design

Across my duller fibre.   And to-day

The shining strip is rent; the exquisite

Fine pattern is destroyed; part of your heart

Aches in my breast; part of my heart lies chilled

In the damp earth with you.   I have been torn

In two, and suffer for the rest of me.

What is my life to me?   And what am I

To life,—a ship whose star has guttered out?

A Fear that in the deep night starts awake

Perpetually, to find its senses strained

Against the taut strings of the quivering air,

Awaiting the return of some dread chord?

Dark, Dark, is all I find for metaphor;

All else were contrast,—save that contrast's wall

Is down, and all opposed things flow together

Into a vast monotony, where night

And day, and frost and thaw, and death and life,

Are synonyms.   What now—what now to me

Are all the jabbering birds and foolish flowers

That clutter up the world?   You were my song!

Now, let discord scream!   You were my flower!

Now let the world grow weeds!   For I shall not

Plant things above your grave—(the common balm

Of the conventional woe for its own wound!)

Amid sensations rendered negative

By your elimination stands to-day,

Certain, unmixed, the element of grief;

I sorrow; and I shall not mock my truth

With travesties of suffering, nor seek

To effigy its incorporeal bulk

In little wry-faced images of woe.

I cannot call you back; and I desire

No utterance of my immaterial voice.

I cannot even turn my face this way

Or that, and say, "My face is turned to you";

I know not where you are, I do not know

If heaven hold you or if earth transmute,

Body and soul, you into earth again;

But this I know:—not for one second's space

Shall I insult my sight with visionings

Such as the credulous crowd so eager-eyed

Beholds, self-conjured in the empty air.

Let the world wail!   Let drip its easy tears!

My sorrow shall be dumb!

—What do I say?

God! God!—God pity me!   Am I gone mad

That I should spit upon a rosary?

Am I become so shrunken?   Would to God

I too might feel that frenzied faith whose touch

Makes temporal the most enduring grief;

Though it must walk awhile, as is its wont,

With wild lamenting!   Would I too might weep

Where weeps the world and hangs its piteous
     wreaths

For its new dead!   Not Truth, but Faith, it is

That keeps the world alive.   If all at once

Faith were to slacken,—that unconscious faith
Which must, I know, yet be the corner-stone
Of all believing,—birds now flying fearless
Across would drop in terror to the earth;
Fishes would drown; and the all-governing reins
Would tangle in the frantic hands of God
And the worlds gallop headlong to destruction!

O God, I see it now, and my sick brain
Staggers and swoons! How often over me
Flashes this breathlessness of sudden sight
In which I see the universe unrolled
Before me like a scroll and read thereon
Chaos and Doom, where helpless planets whirl
Dizzily round and round and round and round,

Like tops across a table, gathering speed

With every spin, to waver on the edge

One instant—looking over—and the next

To shudder and lurch forward out of sight—

*   *   *   *   *   *

Ah, I am worn out—I am wearied out—

It is too much—I am but flesh and blood,

And I must sleep. Though you were dead again,

I am but flesh and blood, and I must sleep.

THE SUICIDE

"Curse thee, Life, I will live with thee no more!

Thou hast mocked me, starved me, beat my body

    sore!

And all for a pledge that was not pledged by me,

I have kissed thy crust and eaten sparingly

That I might eat again, and met thy sneers

With deprecations, and thy blows with tears,—

Aye, from thy glutted lash, glad, crawled away,

As if spent passion were a holiday!

And now I go. Nor threat, nor easy vow

Of tardy kindness can avail thee now

With me, whence fear and faith alike are flown;

Lonely I came, and I depart alone,

And know not where nor unto whom I go;

But that thou canst not follow me I know."

Thus I to Life, and ceased; but through my brain

My thought ran still, until I spake again:

"Ah, but I go not as I came,—no trace

Is mine to bear away of that old grace

I brought! I have been heated in thy fires,

Bent by thy hands, fashioned to thy desires,

Thy mark is on me! I am not the same

Nor ever more shall be, as when I came.

Ashes am I of all that once I seemed.

In me all's sunk that leapt, and all that dreamed

Is wakeful for alarm,—oh, shame to thee,

For the ill change that thou hast wrought in me,

Who laugh no more nor lift my throat to sing!

Ah, life, I would have been a pleasant thing

To have about the house when I was grown

If thou hadst left my little joys alone!

I asked of thee no favor save this one:

That thou wouldst leave me playing in the sun!

And this thou didst deny, calling my name

Insistently, until I rose and came.

I saw the sun no more.—It were not well

So long on these unpleasant thoughts to dwell,

Need I arise to-morrow and renew

Again my hated tasks, but I am through

With all things save my thoughts and this one night,

So that in truth I seem already quite

Free and remote from thee,—I feel no haste

And no reluctance to depart; I taste
Merely, with thoughtful mien, an unknown draught,
That in a little while I shall have quaffed."

Thus I to Life, and ceased, and slightly smiled,
Looking at nothing; and my thin dreams filed
Before me one by one till once again
I set new words unto an old refrain:

"Treasures thou hast that never have been mine!
Warm lights in many a secret chamber shine
Of thy gaunt house, and gusts of song have blown
Like blossoms out to me that sat alone!
And I have waited well for thee to show
If any share were mine,—and now I go!
Nothing I leave, and if I naught attain

33

I shall but come into mine own again!"

Thus I to Life, and ceased, and spake no more,

But turning, straightway, sought a certain door

In the rear wall. Heavy it was, and low

And dark,—a way by which none e'er would go

That other exit had, and never knock

Was heard thereat,—bearing a curious lock

Some chance had shown me fashioned faultily,

Whereof Life held content the useless key,

And great coarse hinges, thick and rough with rust,

Whose sudden voice across a silence must,

I knew, be harsh and horrible to hear,—

A strange door, ugly like a dwarf.—So near

I came I felt upon my feet the chill

Of acid wind creeping across the sill.

THE SUICIDE

So stood longtime, till over me at last
Came weariness, and all things other passed
To make it room; the still night drifted deep
Like snow about me, and I longed for sleep.

But, suddenly, marking the morning hour,
Bayed the deep-throated bell within the tower!
Startled, I raised my head,—and with a shout
Laid hold upon the latch,—and was without.

* * * * * *

Ah, long-forgotten, well-remembered road,
Leading me back unto my old abode,
My father's house! There in the night I came,
And found them feasting, and all things the same
As they had been before. A splendour hung
Upon the walls, and such sweet songs were sung

As, echoing out of very long ago,

Had called me from the house of Life, I know.

So fair their raiment shone I looked in shame

On the unlovely garb in which I came;

Then straightway at my hesitancy mocked:

"It is my father's house!" I said and knocked;

And the door opened. To the shining crowd

Tattered and dark I entered, like a cloud,

Seeing no face but his; to him I crept,

And "Father!" I cried, and clasped his knees, and
    wept.

Ah, days of joy that followed! All alone

I wandered through the house. My own, my own,

My own to touch, my own to taste and smell,

All I had lacked so long and loved so well!

None shook me out of sleep, nor hushed my song,

Nor called me in from the sunlight all day long.

I know not when the wonder came to me

Of what my father's business might be,

And whither fared and on what errands bent

The tall and gracious messengers he sent.

Yet one day with no song from dawn till night

Wondering, I sat, and watched them out of sight.

And the next day I called; and on the third

Asked them if I might go,—but no one heard.

Then, sick with longing, I arose at last

And went unto my father,—in that vast

Chamber wherein he for so many years

Has sat, surrounded by his charts and spheres.

"Father," I said, "Father, I cannot play

The harp that thou didst give me, and all day
I sit in idleness, while to and fro
About me thy serene, grave servants go;
And I am weary of my lonely ease.
Better a perilous journey overseas
Away from thee, than this, the life I lead,
To sit all day in the sunshine like a weed
That grows to naught,—I love thee more than they
Who serve thee most; yet serve thee in no way.
Father, I beg of thee a little task
To dignify my days,—'tis all I ask
Forever, but forever, this denied,
I perish."

   "Child," my father's voice replied,
"All things thy fancy hath desired of me
Thou hast received. I have prepared for thee

Within my house a spacious chamber, where

Are delicate things to handle and to wear,

And all these things are thine. Dost thou love

    song?

My minstrels shall attend thee all day long.

Or sigh for flowers? My fairest gardens stand

Open as fields to thee on every hand.

And all thy days this word shall hold the same:

No pleasure shalt thou lack that thou shalt name.

But as for tasks—" he smiled, and shook his head;

"Thou hadst thy task, and laidst it by," he said.

GOD'S WORLD

O WORLD, I cannot hold thee close enough!

   Thy winds, thy wide grey skies!

   Thy mists, that roll and rise!

Thy woods, this autumn day, that ache and sag

And all but cry with colour! That gaunt crag

To crush! To lift the lean of that black bluff!

World, World, I cannot get thee close enough!

Long have I known a glory in it all,

     But never knew I this;

     Here such a passion is

As stretcheth me apart,—Lord, I do fear

Thou'st made the world too beautiful this year;

My soul is all but out of me,—let fall

No burning leaf; prithee, let no bird call.

AFTERNOON ON A HILL

I WILL be the gladdest thing
　　Under the sun!
I will touch a hundred flowers
　　And not pick one.

I will look at cliffs and clouds
　　With quiet eyes,
Watch the wind bow down the grass,
　　And the grass rise.

And when lights begin to show

Up from the town,

I will mark which must be mine,

And then start down!

SORROW

SORROW like a ceaseless rain
  Beats upon my heart.
People twist and scream in pain,—
Dawn will find them still again;
This has neither wax nor wane,
  Neither stop nor start.

People dress and go to town;
  I sit in my chair.
All my thoughts are slow and brown:
Standing up or sitting down
Little matters, or what gown
  Or what shoes I wear.

TAVERN

I'LL keep a little tavern
  Below the high hill's crest,
Wherein all grey-eyed people
  May set them down and rest.

There shall be plates a-plenty,
  And mugs to melt the chill
Of all the grey-eyed people
  Who happen up the hill.

There sound will sleep the traveller,
  And dream his journey's end,

44

TAVERN

But I will rouse at midnight
  The falling fire to tend.

Aye, 'tis a curious fancy—
  But all the good I know
Was taught me out of two grey eyes
  A long time ago.

ASHES OF LIFE

Love has gone and left me and the days are all alike;

    Eat I must, and sleep I will,—and would that

        night were here!

But ah!—to lie awake and hear the slow hours

    strike!

    Would that it were day again!—with twilight

        near!

Love has gone and left me and I don't know what

    to do;

    This or that or what you will is all the same

    to me;

But all the things that I begin I leave before I'm
  through,—
  There's little use in anything as far as I can see.

Love has gone and left me,—and the neighbors
  knock and borrow,
  And life goes on forever like the gnawing of a
  mouse,—
And to-morrow and to-morrow and to-morrow and
  to-morrow
  There's this little street and this little house.

THE LITTLE GHOST

I KNEW her for a little ghost
    That in my garden walked;
The wall is high—higher than most—
    And the green gate was locked.

And yet I did not think of that
    Till after she was gone—
I knew her by the broad white hat,
    All ruffled, she had on.

By the dear ruffles round her feet,
    By her small hands that hung

In their lace mitts, austere and sweet,

    Her gown's white folds among.

I watched to see if she would stay,

    What she would do—and oh!

She looked as if she liked the way

    I let my garden grow!

She bent above my favourite mint

    With conscious garden grace,

She smiled and smiled—there was no hint

    Of sadness in her face.

She held her gown on either side

    To let her slippers show,

And up the walk she went with pride,
  The way great ladies go.

And where the wall is built in new
  And is of ivy bare
She paused—then opened and passed through
  A gate that once was there.

KIN TO SORROW

AM I kin to Sorrow,
   That so oft
Falls the knocker of my door-
   Neither loud nor soft,
But as long accustomed,
   Under Sorrow's hand?
Marigolds around the step
   And rosemary stand,
And then comes Sorrow—
   And what does Sorrow care
For the rosemary
   Or the marigolds there?

51

Am I kin to Sorrow?

  Are we kin?

That so oft upon my door—

  Oh, come in!

THREE SONGS OF SHATTERING

I

THE first rose on my rose-tree

    Budded, bloomed, and shattered;

During sad days when to me

    Nothing mattered.

Grief of grief has drained me clean;

    Still it seems a pity

No one saw,—it must have been

    Very pretty.

II

Let the little birds sing;
   Let the little lambs play;
Spring is here; and so 'tis spring;—
   But not in the old way!

I recall a place
   Where a plum-tree grew;
There you lifted up your face,
   And blossoms covered you.

If the little birds sing,
   And the little lambs play,
Spring is here; and so 'tis spring—
   But not in the old way!

III

All the dog-wood blossoms are underneath the tree!

Ere spring was going—ah, spring is gone!

And there comes no summer to the like of you and

me,—

Blossom time is early, but no fruit sets on.

All the dog-wood blossoms are underneath the tree,

Browned at the edges, turned in a day;

And I would with all my heart they trimmed a

mound for me,

And weeds were tall on all the paths that led

that way!

THE SHROUD

DEATH, I say, my heart is bowed
   Unto thine,—O mother!
This red gown will make a shroud
   Good as any other!

(I, that would not wait to wear
   My own bridal things,
In a dress dark as my hair
   Made my answerings.

I, to-night, that till he came
   Could not, could not wait,

In a gown as bright as flame
    Held for them the gate.)

Death, I say, my heart is bowed
    Unto thine,—O mother!
This red gown will make a shroud
    Good as any other!

THE DREAM

Love, if I weep it will not matter,
  And if you laugh I shall not care;
Foolish am I to think about it,
  But it is good to feel you there.

Love, in my sleep I dreamed of waking,—
  White and awful the moonlight reached
Over the floor, and somewhere, somewhere
  There was a shutter loose,—it screeched!

Swung in the wind,—and no wind blowing!—
  I was afraid, and turned to you,

Put out my hand to you for comfort,—

And you were gone! Cold, cold as dew,

Under my hand the moonlight lay!

Love, if you laugh I shall not care,

But if I weep it will not matter,—

Ah, it is good to feel you there!

INDIFFERENCE

I SAID,—for Love was laggard, O, Love was slow
to come,—

"I'll hear his step and know his step when I am
warm in bed;

But I'll never leave my pillow, though there be
some

As would let him in—and take him in with tears!"
I said.

I lay,—for Love was laggard, O, he came not until
dawn,—

I lay and listened for his step and could not get
to sleep;

And he found me at my window with my big
cloak on,

All sorry with the tears some folks might weep!

WITCH-WIFE

SHE is neither pink nor pale,
   And she never will be all mine;
She learned her hands in a fairy-tale,
   And her mouth on a valentine.

She has more hair than she needs;
   In the sun 'tis a woe to me!
And her voice is a string of colored beads
   Or steps leading into the sea.

She loves me all that she can,
   And her ways to my ways resign;
But she was not made for any man,
   And she never will be all mine.

BLIGHT

HARD seeds of hate I planted
    That should by now be grown,—
Rough stalks, and from thick stamens
    A poisonous pollen blown,
And odors rank, unbreathable,
    From dark corollas thrown!

At dawn from my damp garden
    I shook the chilly dew;
The thin boughs locked behind me
    That sprang to let me through;

BLIGHT

The blossoms slept,—I sought a place
   Where nothing lovely grew.

And there, when day was breaking,
   I knelt and looked around:
The light was near, the silence
   Was palpitant with sound;
I drew my hate from out my breast
   And thrust it in the ground.

Oh, ye so fiercely tended,
   Ye little seeds of hate!
I bent above your growing
   Early and noon and late,
Yet are ye drooped and pitiful,—
   I cannot rear ye straight!

BLIGHT

The sun seeks out my garden,

No nook is left in shade,

No mist nor mold nor mildew

Endures on any blade,

Sweet rain slants under every bough:

Ye falter, and ye fade.

WHEN THE YEAR GROWS OLD

I CANNOT but remember

　　When the year grows old—

October—November—

　　How she disliked the cold!

She used to watch the swallows

　　Go down across the sky,

And turn from the window

　　With a little sharp sigh.

And often when the brown leaves

　　Were brittle on the ground,

And the wind in the chimney
　　Made a melancholy sound.

She had a look about her
　　That I wish I could forget—
The look of a scared thing
　　Sitting in a net!

Oh, beautiful at nightfall
　　The soft spitting snow!
And beautiful the bare boughs
　　Rubbing to and fro!

But the roaring of the fire,
　　And the warmth of fur,

And the boiling of the kettle

    Were beautiful to her!

I cannot but remember

    When the year grows old—

October—November—

    How she disliked the cold!

SONNETS

I

Thou art not lovelier than lilacs,—no,

 Nor honeysuckle; thou art not more **fair**

 Than small white single poppies,—I can bear

Thy beauty; though I bend before thee, though

From left to right, not knowing where to go,

 I turn my troubled eyes, nor here nor there

 Find any refuge from thee, yet I swear

So has it been with mist,—with moonlight so.

Like him who day by day unto his draught

 Of delicate poison adds him one drop more

Till he may drink unharmed the death of ten,

Even so, inured to beauty, who have quaffed

 Each hour more deeply than the hour before,

I drink—and live—what has destroyed some men.

68

II

Time does not bring relief; you all have lied
  Who told me time would ease me of my pain!
  I miss him in the weeping of the rain;
I want him at the shrinking of the tide;
The old snows melt from every mountain-side,
  And last year's leaves are smoke in every lane;
  But last year's bitter loving must remain
Heaped on my heart, and my old thoughts abide!

There are a hundred places where I fear
  To go,—so with his memory they brim!
And entering with relief some quiet place
Where never fell his foot or shone his face
I say, "There is no memory of him here!"
  And so stand stricken, so remembering him!

69

Mindful of you the sodden earth in spring.

    And all the flowers that in the springtime grow,

    And dusty roads, and thistles, and the slow

Rising of the round moon, all throats that sing

The summer through, and each departing wing,

    And all the nests that the bared branches show,

    And all winds that in any weather blow,

And all the storms that the four seasons bring.

You go no more on your exultant feet

    Up paths that only mist and morning knew,

Or watch the wind, or listen to the beat

    Of a bird's wings too high in air to view,—

But you were something more than young and sweet

    And fair,—and the long year remembers you.

IV

Not in this chamber only at my birth—
　　When the long hours of that mysterious night
　　Were over, and the morning was in sight—
I cried, but in strange places, steppe and firth
I have not seen, through alien grief and mirth;
　　And never shall one room contain me quite
　　Who in so many rooms first saw the light,
Child of all mothers, native of the earth.

So is no warmth for me at any fire
　　To-day, when the world's fire has burned so low;
I kneel, spending my breath in vain desire,
At that cold hearth which one time roared so strong
And straighten back in weariness, and long
　　To gather up my little gods and go.

V

If I should learn, in some quite casual way,

  That you were gone, not to return again—

Read from the back-page of a paper, say,

  Held by a neighbor in a subway train,

How at the corner of this avenue

  And such a street (so are the papers filled)

A hurrying man—who happened to be you—

  At noon to-day had happened to be killed,

I should not cry aloud—I could not cry

  Aloud, or wring my hands in such a place—

I should but watch the station lights rush by

  With a more careful interest on my face,

Or raise my eyes and read with greater care

· Where to store furs and how to treat the hair

VI

BLUEBEARD

THIS door you might not open, and you did;
　So enter now, and see for what slight thing
You are betrayed. . . . Here is no treasure hid,
　No cauldron, no clear crystal mirroring
The sought-for truth, no heads of women slain
　For greed like yours, no writhings of distress,
But only what you see. . . . Look yet again—
　An empty room, cobwebbed and comfortless.
Yet this alone out of my life I kept
　Unto myself, lest any know me quite;
And you did so profane me when you crept
　Unto the threshold of this room to-night
That I must never more behold your face.
　This now is yours. I seek another place.